THE DRUG ABUSE PREVENTION LIBRARY

COCAINE

Rhoda McFarland

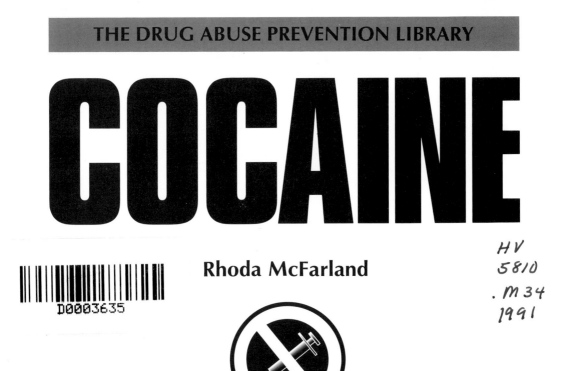

THE ROSEN PUBLISHING GROUP, INC.
NEW YORK

Published in 1991 by The Rosen Publishing Group, Inc.
29 East 21st Street, New York, NY 10010

First Edition

Manufactured in the United States of America

Library of Congress Cataloging-in-Publication Data

McFarland, Rhoda
     Cocaine/Rhoda McFarland—1st ed.
     (The Drug Abuse Prevention Library)
     Includes bibliographical references and index.
     Summary: Examines the harmful effects of cocaine use and addiction, and explains the dangers of teenage drug abuse in general.
        ISBN 0-8239-1264-7
        1. Cocaine habit--Juvenile literature. 2. Cocaine habit--United States--Juvenile literature.
        3. Teenagers--United States--Drug Use--Juvenile literature. [1. Cocaine. 2. Drug Abuse.]
     I. Title II. Series
     HV5810. M34   1991
     362.29 8--dc20   90-45105
                                   CIP
                                   AC

Contents

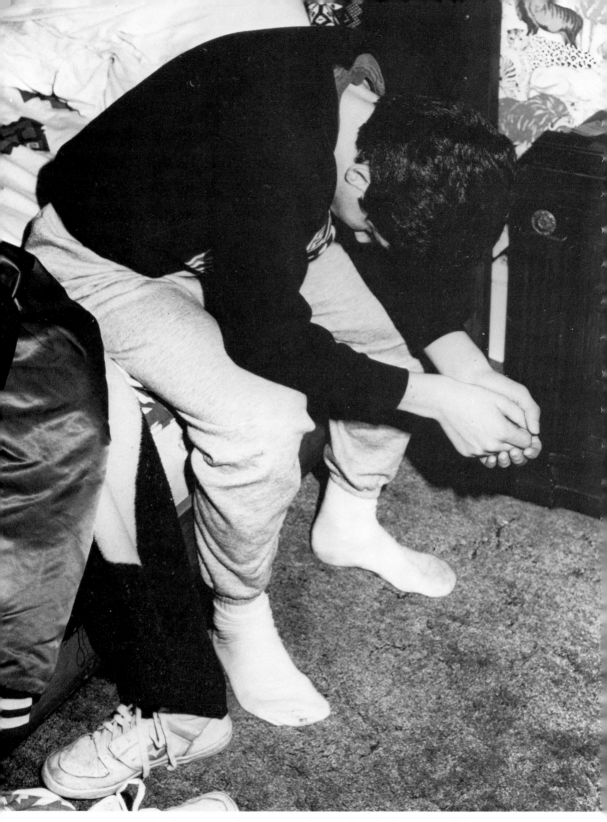

The depression that comes when a drug high wears off drives
many teens to get high again and again.

CHAPTER 1

What Is Drug Dependency?

"It's easy to tell a drug addict. They're always stoned." "You can use drugs once in a while. You won't get hooked." "You snort cocaine twice and you're gone." "You can't get addicted to marijuana." What is true? Drug addicts aren't always stoned. Many people are addicted long before they stay high all the time. You may be able to snort cocaine twice without getting hooked. Then, again, it may not take more than that to get you on the cocaine merry-go-round. And, yes, you can get addicted to marijuana. You need to have facts to answer your questions. What is drug abuse? What is drug dependency? Who is a drug addict?

7

8   Drug abuse is the use of any drug to the point that it causes problems in your life. They can be health problems or money problems. Drug abuse can cause fights with friends or family. There may be problems at school. You become dependent when your mind tells you that you must have the drug. This is *psychological dependence.* You are dependent when your body is uncomfortable without the drug. That is *physical dependence.* Psychological dependence usually happens first.

Another sign of dependence is called *tolerance.* Tolerance means that you must take more of the drug to get the feeling you want. You might hear someone say, "I used to get high on two beers. Now I have to drink four to feel anything."

As dependence grows, you begin to lose control of how much of the drug you use. You will use all you have and look for more. The drug will control you. You will be addicted. Addiction is using a substance without control and continuing no matter what happens to you or others.

People addicted to drugs will do anything to get their drug. They will lie and steal. They will hurt others. They leave their friends. They do things that cause them to get in trouble at home, at school, and with the law. They seem to be bad, evil, or just too weak to break their bad habit. That is not the case at all. Addicts are very ill. They have the disease of *chemical dependence.*

Not everyone who drinks or uses other *mind-altering* drugs becomes dependent. No one knows exactly what causes some people to become addicted while others do not. People with alcoholic parents are 400 times more likely to become addicted to alcohol and other drugs. Chemical dependence runs in families.

Even if your parents do not use any drugs, you may still be at risk. Dependence in any member of your family—grandparents, uncles, aunts, cousins, brothers, or sisters—is a sign for you to be careful.

What Are the Signs of Addiction?

You do not have to be drunk or stoned all the time to be addicted. Addiction has to do with getting the drug, using the drug, and trying to live a normal life. It's not how much you drink or use or how often you drink or use. It's what happens to you when you use. You can ask yourself or your friends the following questions. They

10 are signs that you may be in trouble with chemicals.

- Do you get into fights when you drink or use?
- Do your friends have to tell you what you did because you don't remember? That is called a *blackout.* It is a very serious warning sign that you are in trouble with chemicals.
- Do you say you aren't going to get drunk and then you do?
- Have you ever felt sick while using but kept on using?
- Do you gulp down the first few drinks?
- Do you want an extra hit to get you going?
- Have your friends said you are drinking or using too much?
- Do you often think about drinking or using?
- Do you talk about partying and getting loaded?
- Have your grades been going down?
- Are you having more problems with your parents?
- Have you ever felt guilty about something you did when you were high?
- Do you lie about how much you use?
- Do you drink or use to help you forget your problems?

When you become dependent on a drug you spend a lot of time worrying about where you will get more.

- Do you ever drink or use alone?

A *yes* answer to any of the questions means that chemicals are causing problems in your life. It is a warning sign that you are becoming dependent. It's time to say "No" before you can't say "No." As Mark Gold says in his book, *The Facts about Drugs and Alcohol,* "Use...leads to...tolerance...leads to...abuse...leads to...chemical dependence and addiction." **11**

A step on the road to dependency is cutting school and hanging out with a gang of users.

CHAPTER 2

Facts about Teen Drug Abuse

*T*he drug explosion began in the 1960s. Most drug users were college age or older. Today, many drug users are in their teens. Studies show that the age for first drug use is 11 to 13. The drugs first abused are usually alcohol and tobacco. Studies also show that young people who smoke cigarettes or drink are more likely to use *illegal* drugs. That is why tobacco and alcohol are called gateway drugs. They "open the gate" to the use of other drugs.

The most used illegal drug is marijuana. Getting high on marijuana often makes you want to find out how the others make you feel. There are all kinds of *uppers, downers,* and mixtures to try. What people

13

14 don't talk about is the harm that drugs do to a teen's body. Drugs keep young bodies from growing and developing as they should. Young brains may be damaged. Teen bodies show the effects of drug use quicker than adults.

Besides the illegal drugs, it's easy to get legal *prescription* drugs. Sleeping pills and *tranquilizers* are found in medicine cabinets at home. The most common tranquilizers are Valium and Librium. You may think they just make you feel mellow. Addiction develops very quickly. The *withdrawal* effects don't show up until seven to 10 days after use is stopped. People think they have safely stopped but feel frightened and nervous days later. They can't sleep. They are anxious and jumpy and can't sit still. These feelings can go on for a long time. Medical help is needed.

Stages in Teenage Addiction
The disease of addiction gets worse the longer drugs are used. The more teens use, the more trouble they get into. The disease goes through four stages.

Stage 1 Experimentation
This stage often begins in junior high school. It's the time when everyone is

"trying it." It usually begins with beer drinking, pot smoking, or sniffing an *inhalant*. Hanging out during the summer is when many young teens start getting high.

During the experimental stage, teens have a very low tolerance. It doesn't take much to get high. A few sniffs, a beer, two hits on a *joint* will make a new user feel good. Because they like the way it feels, teens decide to use again.

Stage 2 Tolerance

As someone uses more often, tolerance develops. "I can maintain," people say. Being able to drink more or smoke more than others is something to brag about.

As drug use becomes more important, school becomes less important. Grades go down. Teen users begin to have trouble with teachers, principals, and other students. They lose interest in school sports, clubs, music groups, and such.

There is trouble at home with parents. Users want to party all weekend, staying out all night and sleeping all day. Sometimes they don't go home all weekend.

Drinking and using other drugs during the week begins. The teens may be getting loaded before school in the morning. Having a drink or a smoke at lunch time

16 starts. This is the time when experimenting with other drugs begins. The goal is to get a "better" high with cocaine, *crack, PCP,* or whatever drug is handy.

At the end of this stage, teen users think about using most of the time. How to get drugs, where, when, and with whom to use are most important. At this point the teen may not be addicted but is very harmfully involved.

Stage 3 Addiction

Getting high becomes number one in the teen user's life. Grades go from bad to failing. Often during this stage teen users drop out of school. They do anything to get their drug supply. Lying becomes a way of life. In this stage most users find that stealing and dealing are the best ways to keep supplied. Girls often use sex to get drugs.

Drugs become so important that users don't care about anything else. They feel tired and don't have much energy. They don't care how they look. They have bad fights at home and get in trouble with the law. They do things they know are wrong, and their *self-esteem* goes down. They don't tie in any of their problems with their drug

Even young children learn from their parents that abuse of alcohol is okay.

18 use. They only remember that drugs make them feel good.

As the drug use gets more out of control, users feel guilty. They can't stop even when they try. They feel ashamed because they can't control their use. That makes them use even more. It goes around and around.

Self-help groups enable parents to learn the dangers of drug addiction.

Stage 4 Dependency

The teenagers are addicted to everything and anything. They will drink anything, snort, sniff, smoke, and, finally, shoot up. They use before school, during school, and after school. Dropouts just hang out and stay high most of the time.

By this time, teens no longer use to feel good. They use to feel normal. Families and friends try to help. Nothing works. Some families give up and finally throw them out. They spend time in jail for crimes they do to get drugs. They have no one but their using friends. They get sick easily. They hate themselves so much that they think about suicide. They don't know how to get help. If they don't get help, they will die.

Stopping the Disease

Today there is treatment for addiction. Parents are learning about drug addiction and getting help for teens before it is too late. Courts are sending teens to treatment centers. Addiction can't be cured but can be stopped.

Many teens start smoking because they think it makes them look cool and grown-up.

CHAPTER 3

Why Teens Use Drugs

*J*ack and Jane User use drugs because it makes them feel good. Jane says it's fun. Jack says it's cool. They say it makes them forget about their troubles. Besides, all their friends do drugs. Only nerds are straight. What's going on with Jacks and Janes who turn on to drugs? What makes them look for something to feel good?

Everyone wants to feel loved and accepted. If your parents set very high goals for you, it seems that nothing you do is ever good enough. You never get praised for the high grades. You get ragged on for the low ones. Teachers push you to do better. It seems that no one is ever pleased with what you do.

22   Disapproval of parents and problems at school make you feel bad about yourself. You feel tense and uncomfortable. Gloomy thoughts bring feelings of *depression*. You want to feel better and forget what makes you feel bad. Many teens turn to drugs.

What friends think of you is very important. Friends may pressure you to try drugs. You don't want your friends to think you're afraid. You may think they won't like you if you don't drink that beer or smoke that joint. Being accepted by your friends becomes more important than what your parents think. It can be more important than what *you* think.

The fear of not being accepted makes you feel shy and unsure of yourself. Some teens find that drugs "loosen them up." They don't feel shy when they're loaded.

Some teens use drugs to get back at parents. They know drugs are illegal and parents disapprove of their use. When they get in trouble at school, at home, or with the law, teen users blame their parents.

Some just want to know what it's like. They get caught up in the disease of addiction before they know what's going on.

Boredom leads to drug use. Lots of teens say there's nothing else to do.

In some homes drug use is accepted and approved. Parents who drink and use other drugs see nothing wrong with their children's using. Many give alcohol and other drugs to their children. If there is chemical dependence in your family, your chances of being chemically dependent are very high.

An afternoon with friends can have fun and excitement without involving drugs.

24   All people who are dependent on alcohol or other drugs feel bad about themselves. Whatever the reason for the bad feelings, drugs seem to be a way to feel better. What feels good now can lead to lots of feeling bad later.

It's Easy to Get Started Using Drugs

Most teens start using drugs at home. Early drinking is usually done at home with the family. Later on, most drinking is done away from home. Alcohol is very easy to get. Often it's stolen from parents. Teens stand outside the liquor store or all-night mini-mart and ask adults to buy beer or liquor for them. There's always someone who will.

Usually, friends give you your first marijuana or other illegal drug. At first, everyone chips in to buy drugs. It starts out being fairly cheap to use. After your tolerance builds, you need more. Then costs go up and up. Some dealers sell drugs cheap at first to get you hooked.

It's easy to get a drug. If it isn't sold in the school, someone knows how to get it. Everybody knows where to get "stuff."

Stars Make It Seem Attractive 25

Using alcohol and marijuana is common in movies. It's as if it's no big deal. Rock groups sing about drugs. In the 1970s Eric Clapton sang the song *Cocaine*. The song tells the listener that at the end of the day you look forward to doing cocaine. It says that cocaine is what you do when you are feeling blue so that you will feel better. Motley Crue sang *Dr. Feelgood* in 1989. That song relates a story about a young drug dealer named Rattailed Jimmy who sells cocaine to a group of Mexicans. They call him Dr. Feelgood because he sells them the drugs that make them feel alright. Songs like those make drugs seem good. The singers are successful and looked up to.

There are many reasons why teens use drugs. Some look to drugs for answers. They don't find answers. They find more problems. You can find support and stay drug–free.

Cocaine is mixed with other substances and dried into a paste.

Cocaine

*F*or hundreds of years in South America the Indians of Peru and Bolivia have chewed *coca* leaves. They live high in the Andes Mountains. Chewing coca leaves gives them energy. They can work hard in the high altitude and need little food.

In the late 1700s the coca plant reached Europe. In 1855 *cocaine* was first made. It was used as a medicine and a pleasure drug. In 1884 *Sigmund Freud* wrote a paper telling about the effects of cocaine on himself. He told ways to use the drug that proved unsafe. The only safe and proper medical use for cocaine that Freud found was as a painkiller. Dentists, eye surgeons, and nose and throat doctors

28 | used it as a *local anesthetic.* Later, better local anesthetics were found. Other doctors, believing Freud, gave cocaine to people for almost anything. It was used for seasickness, head colds, and "tired blood." It was the magic cure of the day.

At that time cocaine was cheap, and people could get all they wanted. It was in medicines on drugstore shelves. In 1885 a "health drink" called Coca-Cola was made using small amounts of cocaine. It stayed in the drink until 1905. By that time people were speaking out against cocaine. Doctors broke off their love affair with cocaine when people became ill and even died from cocaine poisoning. The Pure Food and Drug Act of 1906 controlled the use of cocaine. Then it was legal only for medical use.

The illegal use of cocaine went on. Only a few people used it because it became very expensive. In the 1960s the attitude toward illegal drug use began to change. More people began using drugs. With the drug door open, it wasn't long until cocaine came in.

Today the Indians of Peru and Bolivia still chew coca leaves. Most of the coca in the world is grown in those countries. The Indians used to grow coca for their own

Cocaine is seized by the thousands of pounds in the jungles of Bolivia.

use and their religious ceremonies. Drug traffickers wanted the Indians to grow coca for them. They forced the Indians to stop growing their usual crops and grow coca. The Indians made so much money from growing coca that they willingly stopped growing food crops. Now their lives have completely changed. They buy

30 | things they used to make themselves. They eat canned vegetables instead of fresh ones from their fields. They cut down the forest to grow coca.

The Indians have learned to make coca paste. Coca leaves are mixed with *kerosene* and dried in the sun. That makes a yellow paste. Some of the paste is smoked by the Indians. Some is sent to cities where it's smoked. Most of it is sent by plane to Colombia, where it is made into a powdered cocaine. Then the cocaine is shipped to the United States and other parts of the world.

Seventy percent of the cocaine production in the world is controlled by a dozen drug "families" in Colombia. They control the growing and making of coca paste. The families run the labs that make the cocaine and control the shipping of cocaine throughout the world. They pay off government officials in Central America and the Caribbean islands so their cocaine shipments can pass safely through countries. The drug "lords" make billions of dollars. They kill anyone who gets in their way.

Most of the cocaine comes into the U.S. by sea and by plane. The Colombian drug lords often own the planes and the boats.

Between 1981 and 1988 the U.S. government spent $20 billion fighting the drug war. The government uses boats, planes, and radar balloons to stop traffickers from bringing cocaine into the country from the islands of the Caribbean. Government agents also patrol our southern borders where cocaine comes in through Mexico from South America.

Most cocaine comes into the country through Florida. Drug dealers pick up the pure cocaine. Before they sell it, they "cut" it. Sugars, PCP, *Benzocaine, speed,* and even heroin may be mixed in. Street cocaine is often only 30% cocaine. The dealer's pure cocaine goes a long way. That makes the street value (what cut cocaine is worth on the street) very high. That's how dealers make so much money.

Drug addicts forget all the needs of life until they end up as derelicts on city streets.

CHAPTER 5

Facts about Cocaine

*I*n experiments, monkeys that were allowed to have all they wanted took cocaine until they died. People spend all their money, steal, go to jail, lose their home, job, and family and still use cocaine. There is something very powerful about this drug.

Cocaine is a strong *central nervous system stimulant*. It speeds up the work of the body. It affects the part of the brain that brings strong feelings of pleasure. It gives users a wonderful sense of well-being. They feel powerful and have great energy. They no longer feel tired or hungry.

A few minutes after snorting coke the high begins. It peaks in 15 to 20 minutes.

33

34 The effects are gone within an hour. When the effects wear off, the "crash" comes. Users feel depressed, irritable, and tired. Because of the powerful high followed by the deep low, the user wants the drug to make him feel good again. There is a craving for cocaine. That craving causes people to become addicted very quickly.

To get a faster and even stronger high, users take street cocaine and mix it with chemicals to make a paste. They heat the paste and make what is called *freebase.* The freebase is smoked. It's much stronger than snorted cocaine, so the high is greater. It lasts longer, and the crash is worse. Freebasing is even more addicting than snorting. Freebasing can be very dangerous. During heating the chemicals sometimes explode and burn the user.

Using a needle to *inject* or *shoot up* is another way to get a fast high. Cocaine goes into the bloodstream and to the brain very quickly.

Crack

The fastest high comes from *crack.* It is the most addicting form of cocaine. Crack is made by mixing street cocaine with baking soda and water. It's made into small "rocks" that are white to light brown in color. The name comes from the crackling sound the rocks make when they're smoked. The crack high begins in less than 10 seconds. It lasts from 5 to 15 minutes. The high is very high, and the low is very low. The brain is more affected by crack than other forms of cocaine. This causes a drug hunger that doesn't stop. The craving for crack is greater than for any other drug, even heroin. Because of the craving, addiction comes as quickly as two weeks. Most users have major problems within two months.

Crack seems to be very cheap because it can be bought for five or ten dollars. By the gram, crack is almost twice the price of street cocaine. Even though it may seem cheap at first, it does not stay that way. With crack the high is so short that more is needed within a short time. Drug dealers can keep the price of the rocks low because they know users will be back for more and more.

Crack addicts will use until their money or the drug runs out. They can go without eating. They smoke crack until their bodies crash. Within hours of waking up after the crash, the hunger for crack is back.

The high of crack is so much stronger than street cocaine because of the way it's

36 made. Everything in the crack cocaine is made stronger. That means that whatever else is in it is also stronger. If there's PCP or heroin or another form of speed, the user may be in big trouble. Crack is not a purer form of cocaine. It's a stronger form.

Physical Effects of Cocaine

No matter how cocaine is taken, it has two effects. It is an anesthetic and a stimulant. Sniffing cocaine causes the inside of the nose and throat to get numb. It also causes the blood vessels inside the nose to get smaller. The nose gets stuffy or runny. If sniffing goes on for very long, the inside of the nose dries out and cracks and bleeds. Often the cocaine will eat a hole on the inside of the nose. It takes surgery to repair it.

Many cocaine users have very hoarse voices. Cocaine damages their throat. If they stop using in time, their voice returns to normal.

The stimulant effect of cocaine acts quickly on the brain. It changes the chemical makeup in the brain. The chemical change is what causes the craving and quick addiction. Cocaine speeds up the heartbeat and breathing rate. It raises blood pressure and body temperature. Cocaine users don't feel hungry, so they don't eat. They lose weight. Headaches are common, and the eyes are affected. Heavy snorters' eyesight is fuzzy, and they see spots of light called "snow lights." Vomiting and stomach pain are other side effects. Using cocaine in any form often causes *seizures*.

The effects of cocaine on the heart and breathing are very dangerous. You do not have to be a heavy or longtime user to

Drug abuse can lead to violence and injury to both the user and loved ones.

38 | have a heart attack and die. Freebasing and crack are the most likely to lead to heart attacks.

Any cocaine use affects breathing. Smoking coke affects the lungs and throat the most. Heavy coughs bring up *mucus*. It will be dark from crack use. Coughing up dark colored mucus or blood is a sign of lung damage. Any discomfort when breathing is a warning of trouble. Some users die because their lungs fill up with fluid and they can't breathe.

Because they don't eat right, addicts are not healthy. They become sick very easily. Dental problems are common.

There is always a danger of *overdose* and death. Someone can overdose on street cocaine that is purer than usual. Users never know how much pure cocaine is in what they buy. The same amount of a more pure cocaine can kill. Dying from an overdose can happen no matter what way cocaine is used. There is more chance of overdose shooting up. Some people are more likely to be affected than others. Any way they use it could be deadly.

Effects on the Mind

By talking to cocaine addicts, doctors know some of the most common effects of cocaine on the mind. There is a feeling of well-being when high. Then comes depression with the low. Cocaine users think they do everything better when they're high. They can do some easy things very well. They can't do jobs that take thinking. Many users talk a lot when they are high. Most of the time they make no sense at all.

Cocaine users may do the same thing over and over without knowing it. Cocaine causes many users to be angry, get wild, and hurt others. Some feel that everyone is against them, so they stay away from people. They want to be alone. Longtime users begin to see, taste, feel, or smell things that aren't there. At first users claim that sex is better with cocaine. After awhile, they aren't interested in sex and can't do anything about it if they are. Sleep patterns get all mixed up. Users can't sleep or they sleep all the time.

Addiction is the side effect to worry about most. There is no cure and no quick fix. Addiction can be controlled by stopping use of all chemicals. It is very hard to do that without help. With help, staying off drugs is still very hard, especially for cocaine addicts. But it can be done.

Special police units stage raids on known drug dealers' hangouts.

CHAPTER 6

Social Effects of Cocaine Use

*E*veryone is paying for cocaine. Sometimes you pay in dollars through taxes. Other times it costs you the pain of seeing someone you care about destroy himself and his family. You lose your freedom when drug dealers and users make it unsafe for you to be on the streets. All of America is affected by cocaine.

Crime

When cocaine comes in, so does crime. Cities all over the U.S. report higher crime rates because of drugs. Since 1985 when crack came to Washington, D.C., the murder rate has gone from 148 per year to 372. Most of those were crack dealers

41

42 killing other crack dealers. Dealers aren't the only ones getting killed. People who get in their way when they're killing each other get killed too. Cars drive by and spray the neighborhood with bullets. They don't care if they hit someone else. Police all over the country report the connection between cocaine and crime.

Breaking into houses is a way to get money for cocaine. Mugging and robbing people will buy a rock. Stealing and dealing bring in money for cocaine. Girls sell their bodies to get cocaine. So do boys. Starting new users who will be buyers keeps money coming in. Cocaine users use more than cocaine. They use people. Their drug hunger makes then hurt others.

Business

Cocaine costs businesses millions of dollars every year. Workers on cocaine miss work because they get sick more often. When they are at work they can't do their job. Someone on cocaine is more likely to have an accident. That means time away from the job. Users often steal from the company to pay for cocaine.

Many companies understand about addiction. They have special people who deal with workers' problems. Workers in trouble with cocaine or other drugs are sent for treatment. People don't want to lose their jobs. Getting treatment with the help of the company makes people want to stop using forever.

Schools

The anger that goes with cocaine use goes to school with the user. Classrooms become battlegrounds. Users like to give teachers a bad time. They like other kids to think they're tough. Teachers can't give you the time you need. Your education is affected by cocaine.

Because they're angry, users get into fights at school. When they're high, they will fight anyone. When they're coming down, they are often even more dangerous. A cocaine user is a time bomb waiting to go off.

Users are dangerous in other ways too. They bring drugs to school. They try to get others to use. Dropouts hang around school to sell drugs.

Drug users can't work because their brain doesn't work right. Drug–using dropouts become the poor and homeless. Studies show that crack is one of the main reasons why people become homeless. Drug users want help from others, but

44 they never give any help. Society pays because of their use.

Many dropouts leave home. Some are never heard of again. Using cocaine today robs them of their tomorrow.

Disease

Cocaine use is very dangerous to your health. The *contagious* diseases it causes are a problem.

Hepatitis is a disease that is spread by using unclean needles. It is a disease of the liver. You can become very ill and even die. Cocaine shooters often get hepatitis.

Cocaine is a major cause of AIDS. AIDS is another disease spread by using unclean needles. Cocaine users who shoot up don't worry about using clean needles. They just want to get high.

AIDS is also passed during sex. Drug users are known to have many sex partners. You don't have to be a *shooter* to get AIDS. Having sex with a needle user is as dangerous as shooting up yourself. Having sex with anyone who has had sex with shooters or their partners is as dangerous as shooting up yourself. The Centers for Disease Control reported that AIDS in teenagers 13 to 19 went up 40 percent between 1987 and 1989. They expect it to

keep rising because teenagers have so
many sex partners.

Other sexually passed diseases called
venereal diseases (VD) are showing up in
teen drug users. In some parts of the
country where crack use is rising, so are
syphilis and *gonorrhea*. Teens have so
many sex partners that they don't remember them all. Health departments can't
find all of the partners to treat them for
the diseases. The diseases are spreading
like wildfire. Luckily, VD can be cured
with antibiotics. Today there is no cure
for AIDS.

Cocaine Babies

The saddest victims of cocaine addiction
are babies born to addicted mothers. They
are born addicted to cocaine. They must
go through very painful withdrawal after
they are born. They shake and jerk and
cry in pain. They are often born early and
are very small. Many die in their sleep
before their first birthday. Birth defects
are common. Cocaine babies grow and
develop slowly.

As cocaine babies grow older, they have
learning problems. They can't sit still.
They can't pay attention for very long.
They don't get along well with other chil-

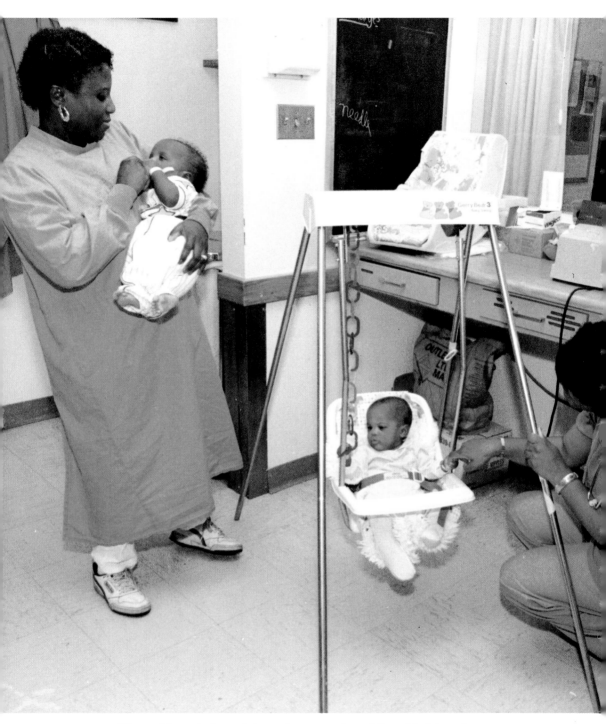

The saddest victims of drug abuse are the addicted babies of
cocaine-abusing mothers.

dren. Schools don't know how to deal with their special needs. Even with special help, it is feared that children born addicted will have major problems in life. Their problems become problems for everyone.

Cocaine and You

You may not use cocaine, but it affects you. You may not think you can do anything about it. You can find others who are troubled about drug use. You can join a group that is drug–free and wants to help others be drug–free. Many towns and cities have groups for teens who want to help younger children. They go to schools and do plays or talk to kids so they won't start using drugs. Find out what's happening and join in. YOU can make a difference.

There are many easy ways to say "No" to "friends" who offer you a joint.

CHAPTER 7

Saying "No" to Drugs

Staying drug–free is not easy. You live in a drug–using country. Real men drink beer. Television's rich have cocktails before dinner, wine with dinner, a few drinks after dinner. Got a headache? "Take a pill." Need to get some sleep? "Take a pill." Feeling uptight? "Have a drink." "Here's a joint." "Don't be such a baby." "Try it. You'll feel great." "Come on, one little *toot* won't kill you." "I thought you were my friend." "What's the matter, you chicken?" "Everybody drinks...smokes a little dope...snorts a line or two...." It's easy to start using, but hard to stop. Not starting is the wise choice, and you need some ways to say "No."

49

50 *Stay Away from Trouble*

If you know people who are users, it's best to stay away from them. When you go someplace where people are using, leave as soon as possible. If you know drugs will be at the party, don't go. Avoid trouble if you can. If you can't, here are some ways to say "No."

Just Say "No"

When someone offers you drugs, say "No" firmly. If it's possible, leave.

"No, thanks."

"I'm not drinking tonight."

"I don't use."

"I'm not interested."

"Forget it."

"No way."

Say "No" and Give a Reason

Most people don't feel comfortable just saying "No." They feel they have to give a reason. If you say "Yes" you don't have to tell why. If you say "No" you don't have to tell why either. If you feel that you must, then have a reason or an excuse ready. There are times when a "little white lie" may save your life, or a joke may get you out of a tight spot.

"Sorry, I have to go see my grand-mother in the hospital."

"No, thanks, it's bad for my heart."

"No, thanks. That stuff will kill you."

"No, thanks. I want to live to see my next birthday."

"I can't today. I've got to go buy some new running shoes."

"Sorry, I have to take my dog to the vet."

"I'm in training for the Ping Pong play-offs."

It's always best to walk away after you've given your reason or excuse. If you stay around to discuss it, they are more likely to talk you into doing what you don't want to do.

Beat Them at Their Own Game

Users will try to make you feel that there's something wrong with you because you don't use. Don't try to change their mind. Beat them at their own game.

"What's the matter, you chicken?

"You got it."

Flap your arms like wings and make chicken noises as you walk away.

"I'd rather be a chicken than a dead duck."

52 When you show you don't care, it takes the power away from them. You're in control.

Many times users will make comments in front of you as though you weren't there.

"That's Sam. His girlfriend won't let him smoke anymore. Big man. Woman runs his life."

At times like that, ignore them and keep walking. They just want to push your buttons. They want you to come down to their level. Stay where you are. You're way above them.

Be a Broken Record

Most people won't listen to your reasons for not using. No reason will be good enough. They want you to change your mind. If you can't leave, try being a broken record until they get tired and leave you alone.

"Come and have a smoke."

"No, thanks, I don't use."

"This is really good stuff."

"No, thanks, I don't use."

"Just try it."

"No, thanks, I don't use."

"What's the matter with you?"

"I don't use."

The other person will run out of things to say long before you do!

Act Surprised

Act as if you can't believe they're asking you to use drugs. Let them know you think they're worth too much to be using drugs.

"I can't believe you do drugs."

"I'm surprised to hear that from you. You're much too good to mess with that stuff."

"You've got too much going for you to use that stuff."

Get Support

With so much pressure to do drugs, you need help to stay drug–free. Many schools have support groups for students who want to stay straight. If not, your school counselor may know about groups in your area. You need to have friends who have fun without using drugs.

Many school districts have special drug education departments. There are Student Assistance Programs. Call and find out if you can help with the program. Call and ask for help for yourself or a friend.

If you have a friend or family member whose drinking or drug use worries you, go to Alateen. Call the AlAnon number in your phone book and ask about Alateen.

If your parents are alcoholic, there may be a special group for children of alcoholics in your area. The National Council on Alcoholism may have a group near you. Their number is in the telephone book.

Any questions you have about cocaine or cocaine users can be answered by calling the Cocaine HOT LINE. The number is 1-800-COCAINE.

If the test in Chapter 1 showed you that you have a problem with alcohol or drugs, see your school counselor. Call Alcoholics Anonymous, Narcotics Anonymous, or Cocaine Anonymous and ask where you can attend a young people's AA, CA or NA group. Look in the yellow pages under Alcoholism and Drug Abuse. Look in the white pages for County Health Department for drug and alcohol services. Look in the Help List at the end of the book.

You will need lots of help. You can't stop all by yourself. You need to talk to your parents about your problem. If you can't tell them about it by yourself, get an adult you can trust to help you. Make that phone call and get the help you need. You can say "NO" to drugs and "YES" to life. You can do it today.

Glossary
Explaining New Words

addiction The need to use a drug, with loss of control and continued use no matter what happens to you or others.

Alcoholics Anonymous (AA) A community group of chemically dependent people who meet together, share their feelings, and help one another to stay well and not drink or use other drugs.

alcoholism An illness that causes people to become dependent on alcohol due to changes in the brain.

amphetamines Stimulant drugs that are often abused.

anesthetic A drug that blocks pain; local anesthetics block pain to a chosen area.

56   **barbiturates** Depressants that are sometimes prescribed to help people sleep or prevent seizures.

Benzocaine A local anesthetic.

blackout Loss of memory of what went on while drinking or using other drugs.

chemical dependence A strong feeling of need for a drug that causes people to keep on taking the drug.

central nervous system The brain, spinal cord, and nerves.

coca The plant from which cocaine is made.

cocaine A powerful central nervous system stimulant taken from the leaves of the coca plant, and usually made into a powder that is sniffed, smoked, or injected.

Cocaine Anonymous (CA) A community group of cocaine addicts who meet together, share their feelings, and help one another to stay well and not use cocaine or other drugs.

compulsive Happening again and again; uncontrolled need to do something again and again.

contagious Tending to spread from person to person.

crack A very dangerous form of cocaine that is smoked.

depressant A mind–altering drug that
slows the work and actions of the body.

downers Street name for depressants.

drug A chemical substance that changes
how the mind or body works.

freebase A form of cocaine that is
smoked.

gonorrhea A venereal disease.

hallucinogens Illegal drugs that cause a
person to see, hear, or feel things that are
not real.

heroin A narcotic.

ice A strong, highly addicting stimulant.

inhalants Products that give off dangerous fumes; sometimes used as drugs by
people who sniff them.

inject To force into the body using a
needle; to give a shot.

illegal Against the law.

joint Marijuana cigarette.

kerosene A white oily liquid usually used
as fuel; may be used to change coca leaves
into coca paste.

mind–altering drugs Drugs that change
or alter the way the brain and nervous
system function, thus affecting the messages to and from the brain.

narcotics Strong depressants that are
prescribed to relieve pain.

58 **Narcotics Anonymous** (NA) A community group of chemically dependent people who meet together, share their feelings, and help one another to stay well and not use drugs.

overdose To take more of a drug than the body can handle.

PCP A strong hallucinogen.

peer Someone your own age.

prescription drugs Medicines that must be ordered by a doctor and prepared by a pharmacist.

physical Having to do with the body.

psychological Having to do with the mind.

seizure An upset in the normal flow of messages from the brain to the rest of the body causing out of control movements or unusual behavior for a short period of time.

self-esteem Your opinion of you; the way you feel about yourself.

shoot up Inject.

shooter Someone who injects drugs.

side effects Unwanted changes in the body that can be caused by taking drugs.

Sigmund Freud The first psychiatrist.

speed A street name for amphetamines.

stimulant A mind–altering drug that speeds up the work of the body.

street value What cut cocaine sells for on the street.

syphilis A venereal disease.

tolerance Needing more of a drug to get the same effect.

toot Street name for cocaine; to sniff cocaine.

tranquilizer A type of depressant given to help people relax when they are under great stress.

uppers Street name for stimulants.

venereal disease Disease spread by having sex with a person who has the disease.

withdrawal The physical signs such as cramps, fever, chills, shaking, and upset stomach that happen when a user stops taking drugs. Psychological signs of withdrawal are feelings of anxiety, fear, confusion, and depression.

Help List

Telephone Book
- Cocaine HOT LINE 1-800-COCAINE

Yellow Pages
- Alcoholism, Drug Abuse, Counselors

White Pages
- Alcoholics Anonymous, AlAnon, Narcotics Anonymous, National Council on Alcoholism, Alcoholism Counseling, Drug Abuse Services, Cocaine Anonymous

Government Listings
- Alcoholism Treatment, Drug Abuse, County Health Services, Child Protective Services

School
- Counselors, school nurse, Drug Education and Student Services, Health Services

Community
- Church
- YMCA
- YWCA

Write or call

• National Association of Children of Alcoholics
31706 Pacific Coast Highway, Suite 20
South Laguna, CA 95677
(714) 499-3889

• National Council on Alcoholism
12 West 21st Street
New York, NY 10010
(212) 206-6770

• AA World Services, Inc.
P.O. Box 459
Grand Central Station
New York, NY 10163

• AlAnon Family Group Headquarters
P.O. Box 182
Madison Square Station
New York, NY 10159

• Narcotics Anonymous
World Service Office
16155 Wyandotte Street
Van Nuys, CA 91406

For Further Reading

Berger, Gilda. *Addiction: Its Causes, Problems and Treatments.* New York: Franklin Watts, 1982.

Chomet, Julian. *Cocaine and Crack.* New York: Franklin Watts, 1987.

Edwards, Gabrielle I. *Coping With Drug Abuse.* New York: The Rosen Publishing Group, 1990 rev. ed.

McFarland, Rhoda. *Coping With Substance Abuse.* New York: The Rosen Publishing Group, 1990, rev. ed.

Shulman, Jeffrey. *Focus on Cocaine and Crack.* Frederick, MD: Twenty-First Century Books, 1990.

Index

About the Author
    Rhoda McFarland has taught all grades kindergarten through twelfth. She is a certified alcoholism and drug abuse counselor having worked with troubled young people and their parents. She developed and implemented the first educational program in the California area for students making the transition from drug/alcohol treatment programs back into the regular school system. She is currently working as a Peace Corp volunteer in Belize, Central America.

Photo Credits
Cover photo: Stuart Rabinowitz
Photos on pages 2,6,11,12,17,18,37: Stuart Rabinowitz; pages 20, 48: Mary Lauzon; page 23: Barbara Kirk; pages 26,29,40,46: AP/ Wide World; page 32: Bruce Glassman.

Design & Production: Blackbirch Graphics, Inc.